YOUR KNOWLEDGE HAS V

- We will publish your bachelor's and master's thesis, essays and papers

- Your own eBook and book - sold worldwide in all relevant shops

- Earn money with each sale

Upload your text at www.GRIN.com
and publish for free

Bibliographic information published by the German National Library:

The German National Library lists this publication in the National Bibliography; detailed bibliographic data are available on the Internet at http://dnb.dnb.de .

Imprint:

Copyright © 2017 GRIN Verlag
Print and binding: Books on Demand GmbH, Norderstedt Germany
ISBN: 9783668712270

This book at GRIN:

https://www.grin.com/document/427001

Harry Kreil

Strategic Political Postures of the Conservatives in the UK General Election 2015 and 2017. Analysis and Comparison

GRIN Verlag

GRIN - Your knowledge has value

Since its foundation in 1998, GRIN has specialized in publishing academic texts by students, college teachers and other academics as e-book and printed book. The website www.grin.com is an ideal platform for presenting term papers, final papers, scientific essays, dissertations and specialist books.

Visit us on the internet:

http://www.grin.com/

http://www.facebook.com/grincom

http://www.twitter.com/grin_com

Individual Assignment - Political Marketing

An analysis and comparison of the Strategic Political Postures of the Conservatives in the UK General Election 2015 and 2017

Author: Harry Kreil

Abstract

This paper is motivated by the growing interest in the strategies that political actors and parties adopt to be successful in the electoral market. This work focuses on the election campaigns of the Conservative party in the United Kingdom´s general elections 2015 and 2017. In particular, it tries to identify which strategic orientation the Conservatives applied in their approach towards the electoral market. The degree of strategic orientation of a party with regard to political marketing management can be operationalized by the deployment of the Strategic Political Posture concept. After the Strategic Political Postures of the Conservative´s 2015 and 2017 election campaign are derived, both postures are compared, in order to make suggestions on possible reasons for a change in strategic orientation.

Introduction

In 2016, the British people decided on the referendum on the membership of the United Kingdom in the European Union which showed that most of the voters favoured to leave the EU. Although the Conservative party, currently the strongest party in Britain, endorsed to stay in the EU, the people decided differently. As a result, the Prime Minister and current leader of the Conservatives, Theresa May, made a call for a snap election in 2017 in order to increase the Conservative's share of seats in the House of Commons and therefore have a stronger position and support of the House of Commons in the upcoming negotiations on the withdrawal from the EU. Given that the Conservatives won more seats in the House of Commons elections in 2015 than most experts had expected, it is surprising that the decision of the constituency in the referendum differed from the propositions of the Conservatives. It is therefore interesting to examine, whether there was a change in strategy, particularly in the Strategic Political Posture of the Conservative party between the 2015 and 2017 general elections.

Course of action

The paper is organised as follows. First of all, the topic is introduced by giving a theoretical overview of the Strategic Political Posture concept and its different specifications. After the theoretical fundament is set, the Strategic Political Postures of the Conservative's party in the United Kingdom general elections 2015 and 2017 are derived and analyzed. In order to discover a possible change in postures, the Strategic Political Postures of 2015 and 2017 are compared in an attempt to find possible reasons for a change.

Strategic Political Postures

To understand the way in which parties and candidates exchange value propositions in the electoral market, it is useful to apply theoretical concepts. Additionally, political actors need to have an overall strategy plan that can be seen as a guideline the party complies with. This helps gaining success in an election campaign through the efficient alignment of its communication instruments (Henneberg, 2006). An appropriate concept to measure the basic orientation of a party or candidate towards the electoral market concerning Political Marketing Management, are the Strategic Political Postures (SPP) (Ormrod & Henneberg, 2006). Henneberg (2006) distinguishes two main dimensions that constitute the different

Strategic Political Postures from which parties or political actors can choose when deciding on a competitive position in the political sphere:

- Leading: When a party tries to lead, they know, that their political offering is substiantially right. This mostly involves trying to actively convince other of the beneficial nature of offering of the party. As a result, Political Marketing Management is only a tactical tool to pursue a certain mission (Ormrod et al., 2013).

- Following: When a party decides to follow, they anticipate or analyze the wishes of their target voters and create an offering that best represents the wishes of the largest possible number of individuals (Ormrod et al., 2013). Following implicates that Political Marketing is not a tool only a tool to execute the parties strategy but is also needed to develop the political offering and therefore the strategic orientation (Henneberg, 2006). Parties, that follow the market, also have to react to "events such as public opinion changes by developing adaptive offerings that fulfill stakeholder's needs and wants" (Ormrod & Henneberg, 2011, S. 7).

Although these dimensions seem to be contradictory, both can be applied at the same time. The degree to which these two dimensions are used simultaneously leads to four specific strategic postures that are illustrated and described in the following section (Ormrod et al., 2013):

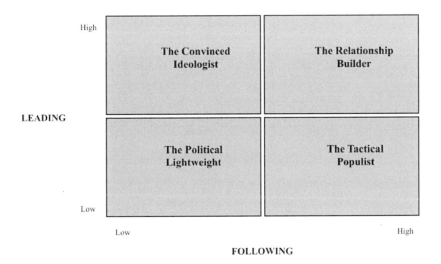

The Convinced Ideologist has a high emphasis on the leading dimension, while following is not aspired. The common characteristic of the Convinced Ideologist is the existence of a focal point, which drives the policy-making, for example a certain ideology or religion. Shifts in public opinions do not have an impact on the policy-making, while the voters should be convinced of the beneficial aspects of the party´s policies. Therefore, political marketing management instruments are mainly used to bring ideologically-driven issues to the fore (Ormrod et al., 2013).

The conceptual antagonist of the Convinced Ideoligist is the Tactical Populist. Tactical Populists take a strong position in following while leading capabilities are not developed. The aim of this strategic orientation is to adapt the political offering to changes in public opinion. Therefore the Tactical Populist has to be flexible in his core offerings (Ormrod et al., 2013).

Parties which pursue high leading and high following dimensions are called Relationship Builders. Parties characterized with this posture focus on long-term relationships rather than transactions. The aim of this strategy is to lock voters into a commitment-trust relationship. The development of the party´s offering is affected by the use of political marketing concepts while simultaneously constituting ideological roots and the long term political beliefs of the party (Ormrod et al., 2013)

The fourth and remaining posture, the Political Lightweight, can be neglected. Low dimensions of both leading and following can be regarded as non-strategy. Therefore, this posture is not taken into account in the further discussion (Ormrod et al., 2013).

Strategic Political Posture of the Conservatives in the 2015 United Kingdom Election

In order to derive the Strategic Political Posture of the Conservative Party, there needs to be measured to which extent the party adopts leading and following dimensions. The best proxy for this dimensions are the manifestos of the Conservative party. The 2015 election campaign´s manifesto title states: "Strong Leadership. A clear economic plan. A brighter, more secure." (Conservative party manifesto, 2015). The title already gives an indication on a stronger leading dimension.

Henneberg (2006) proposes some further indicators, which could lead to a better determination of the following dimension. These indications relate to the party approach in policy making or proposition development, the use of political marketing concepts and instruments and the activities, for which political marketing is applied.

Considering the party´s approach in policy-making, it hast to be outlined that the Conservatives have a natural underlying ideology, namely Conservatism. This ideology serves as a focal point which drives policy-making. Therefore the underlying proposition development of the Conservatives can be regarded as influenced by leading rather than following. This characteristic is mostly assigned to Convinced Ideologist Parties, which perform high in leading and low in following.

To make a judgement on the extent of the use of political marketing concepts and to determine on which activities it was applied, we have to focus on the internal organisation and processes of the Conservative party, which is hard to obtain. However, the manifesto of the Conservative's campaign in 2015 shows no indications, that marketing concepts were used to adapt the proposition to public opinion changes. Also, there is no evidence of activities carried out that pursue a following approach.

Due to the high level of leading and low level of following, the Strategic Political Posture of the Conservatives Party in 2015 can be categorized best as a Convinced Ideologist posture.

Strategic Political Posture of the Conservatives in the 2017 United Kingdom Election

In the 2017 Election campaign, the Conservatives named their manifesto "Forward, together. Our Plan for a Stronger Britain and a Prosperous Future" (Conservative party manifesto, 2017). In contrast to the 2015 manifesto title, there is a remarkable change in semantics, indicating that the focus on leading is either getting weaker or the importance of following is getting higher. Regarding the undeniable historic ideologic roots, lower efforts of leading would contradict the core beliefs of the Conservative party. Therefore, a higher orientation towards following seems more likely. Another aspect that supports this claim, is that the manifesto contains several sections about long term perspectives and common challenges that the British constituency will face in future. This indicates a focus on long-term relationships rather than just a transactional focus on the upcoming election period.

Although the ideologic beliefs of the Conservatives are pro-European, the outcomes of the Referendum on the membership in the European Union were taken into account in the manifesto and a strategy had to be developed on how to deal with these circumstances. This suggests that the Conservatives used marketing concepts to develop the party's offering while simultaneously maintaining their political ideological beliefs. Therefore the Strategical Political Posture of the Conservatives in the 2017 Election can be regarded as a Relationship Builder, which performs high in both leading and following.

Comparison of the Strategic Political Postures of the Conservative Party in the 2015 and 2017 Election

According to the prior sections, the Strategic Political Posture of the Conservatives moved from being a Convinced Ideologist posture in the 2015 election to a Relationship Builder posture in 2017. This is due to a higher orientation towards following in 2017 compared to 2015. This is in line with findings of (Ormrod et al., 2013), who state that parties have developed more following-dominated postures and nowadays there is a stronger emphasis on follower strategies.

One possible reason for the change from Convinced Ideologist to a Relationship Builder might be the outcome of the Referendum on the membership in the European Union in 2016. Although the Conservatives as the strongest party in parliament advocated to remain in the European Union, which is in line with their core beliefs, the constituency decided the United Kingdom leave the European Union. Subsequently, the incumbent leader of the Conservatives and Prime Minister David Cameron, who was re-elected in 2015, resigned and the new Prime Minister and leader was designated, Theresa May. In order to achieve a higher share of seats in the Parliament and thus have more power in the negotiations with the European Union, she pursued to have a snap election, which led to the 2017 Election campaign. As a result of the undesired outcome of the Referendum, the Conservatives may have tried to implement political marketing strategies and tools to better understand and synthesize the needs of the constituency in their policy-making.

Conclusion

Summing up, this paper tried to derive and compare the Strategic Political Postures of the Conservative party in the United Kingdom general election campaigns in 2015 and 2017. After outlining the theoretical framework, the Strategic Political Posture of the Conservatives in the 2015 election campaign was derived as a Convinced Ideologist party, due to high dimensions of leading while disregarding the follower dimension. In contrast, the 2017 election campaign showed a higher orientation towards the follower dimension, therefore categorizing the posture of the Conservatives as a Relationship Builder.

On one hand, this change can be explained by a current general trend of parties moving towards more following-oriented dimensions. On the other hand, the decision of the British constituency to leave the European Union, which contradicted the beliefs of the

Conservatives, might have lead to an urge of integrating public opinion changes in the parties offering.

Finally it has to be mentioned, that these findings might be subjective, because of the "limited rationality based on perceptual bias" (Ormrod et al. 2013, S. 141), due to the complicated analytical process of deriving a Strategic Political Posture.

Literature

Conservative party manifesto (2015): Forward, together. Our Plan for a Stronger Britain and a Prosperous Future. Retrieved July 31, 2017, from https://s3-eu-west-1.amazonaws.com/manifesto2015/ConservativeManifesto2015.pdf

Conservative party manifesto (2017): Forward, together. Our plan for a Stronger Britain and a Prosperous future. Retrieved July 31, 2017, from https://www.conservatives.com/manifesto

Henneberg, S. C. M. (2006): Leading or Following?, In: Journal of Political Marketing, Vol. 5(3), 29–46.

Ormrod, R. P., & Henneberg, S. C. (2006): Different Facets of Market Orientation: A Comparative Analysis of Party Manifestos, In: Journal of Political Marketing, Vol. 8(3), 190–208.

Ormrod, R. P., & Henneberg, S. C. (2011): Political market orientation and strategic party postures in Danish political parties, In: European Journal of Marketing , Vol. 45 (6), 852-881.

Ormrod, R. P., & Henneberg, S. C. , O´ Shaughnessy, N. J. (2013): Political Marketing: Theory and Concepts. London: Sage.

Lightning Source UK Ltd.
Milton Keynes UK
UKRC02n0323231018
331008UK00007B/76